1,000 WAYS

TO BE A

Slightly

BETTER WOMAN

1,000 WAYS

TO BE A

Slightly

BETTER

WOMAN

HOW TO BE thinner, richer, sexier,
kinder, saner, and happier enough

PAMELA REDMOND SATRAN

THE *Glamour List* COLUMNIST

STEWART, TABORI & CHANG
NEW YORK

Published in 2008 by Stewart, Tabori & Chang
An imprint of Harry N. Abrams, Inc.

Library of Congress Cataloging-in-Publication Data

   Satran, Pamela Redmond.
     1,000 ways to be a slightly better woman : how to be thinner, richer, sexier, kinder, saner, and happier enough / Pamela Redmond Satran.
        p. cm.
   Includes bibliographical references.
   ISBN 978-1-58479-671-8
   1. Women—Life skills guides. 2. Women—Psychology. I. Title. II. Title: Thousand ways to be a slightly better woman. III. Title: One thousand ways to be a slightly better woman.

  HQ1221.S294 2008
  646.70082—dc22   2007040599

Editor: Jennifer Levesque
Designer: Michelle Farinella Design
Production Manager: Jacquie Poirier

The text of this book was composed in Eureka.

Printed and bound in the United States of America.
10 9 8 7 6 5 4 3 2 1

HNA ▌▌▌▌▌
harry n. abrams, inc.
a subsidiary of La Martinière Groupe

115 West 18th Street
New York, NY 10011
www.hnabooks.com

ACKNOWLEDGMENTS

I'm a slightly better writer, and this is a much better book, thanks to the help of many people.

At least a couple hundred of the tips in this book were inspired by my ever-brilliant and supportive agent, Deborah Schneider, and my editor Jennifer Levesque, who personifies that magic combination of enthusiasm and grace. Ann Stratton at Stewart, Tabori & Chang contributed several fantastic and original list ideas.

Thank you to Kim Bonnell, my partner in writing *The Glamour List*, for always making the process of list-making fun and fresh, even when I'm doing it without her. Lauren Brody is our terrific list editor at *Glamour*, and editor-in-chief Cindi Leive creates a magazine that makes everyone who works on it—and reads it—slightly better month after month. I started *The Glamour List* column with editor Judy Coyne, who had the idea first and drafted me to make it happen—and whose witty voice I still always hear in my head as I write.

I owe my appreciation to friends and family who generously contributed to specific lists in this book. My well-read son Joe Satran helped distill the Great Books; the brilliant young composer Dennis Tobenski suggested music to calm you down (and rev you up); Rita DiMatteo contributed business and negotiating wisdom; Valerie Frankel, author of the forthcoming memoir *Thin is the New Happy*, suggested ways to stop obsessing about weight; Leslie Brody and Elliot Pinsley passed on transcendent video ideas; and my gorgeous and talented redheaded nieces Georgia and Louisa Oppenheim enlightened me on gifts to thrill any little girl.

CONTENTS

6

95 WAYS TO BE A SEXUAL DEMIGODDESS 74

7

81 WAYS TO LOOK MORE LIKE ANGELINA JOLIE (OR AT LEAST LESS LIKE YOUR AUNT ETHEL) 84

8

86 WAYS TO BE A LESS DESPERATE HOUSEWIFE 98

9

73 WAYS TO RAISE YOUR IQ BY AT LEAST FIVE POINTS 112

10

76 WAYS TO BE A LITTLE MORE SUCCESSFUL AT WORK 126

11 75 WAYS TO ADD DOLLARS TO YOUR NET WORTH 140

12 79 WAYS TO MAKE THE WORLD A SLIGHTLY BETTER PLACE 150

INTRODUCTION

We all want to be better women: thinner, stronger, sexier, more loving, more independent, richer, calmer, more spiritual, better at baking cookies and finding designer clothes at 98% off.

Sometimes. And sometimes we just want to pop another chocolate truffle and tell all those people going on and on (and on) about how much better we should be to give their self-improvement lecture to somebody who needs it. Because we're perfectly perfect exactly the way we are.

Except for those extra three pounds (Okay: eight. Okay: twenty). Except for the pile of clothes on the floor and the alarmingly large Visa bill and the fact that we haven't had time or energy for sex in, oh. . .

Listen, we don't want to talk about it. We do, but we don't want you to bug us. We don't have the time, the energy, the *heart* for a complete overhaul. And we've tried all that super self-help stuff, and we know it just doesn't work, not for long, anyway.

I mean, let's get real. Short of a liposuction machine the size of New Jersey, we're not going to have a totally new body by next Monday. We don't really want to undergo extreme makeovers or undertake new marriages or turn our selves or our lives upside down and inside out.

What we really want to do is tweak: improve at our own pace, in our own way, little by little, leaving enough time left over for a glass of wine and *Desperate Housewives*.

That's what this book offers. Instead of telling you how to look like Paris Hilton, this book tells you how to merely *look* ten pounds thinner—and when the healthiest tack is to eat another chocolate. Instead of exhorting you to be a dynamo in the bedroom, this book tells you how to be a better kisser, when fantasy is as good as the real thing, and exactly what you can yada yada with your man.

And it tells you how to do all those things in easily digestible list form, perfect for the woman (like me and, I suspect, you) who's too busy to wade through 300 pages of dense text to tease out the five or eight or twelve things she really has to do. I started writing lists like the ones in this book for *Glamour* magazine in the nineties, initiating "The Glamour List" column, which I still cowrite with Kimberly Bonnell. One of my lists—Things Every Woman Should Have & Should Know— has even become a popular chain email, attributed to everyone from Hillary Clinton to Maya Angelou and catalogued in Rutgers University's archive of urban myths.

I've written my trademark lists for other magazines too, from *Parenting* to *Redbook* to *Good Housekeeping*, drawing on my experience as a mom and a wife, a working woman and a citizen of the world. The eight baby-naming books I've coauthored with Linda Rosenkrantz, including *Beyond Jennifer & Jason* and *Cool Names for Babies*, all hinge on lists as a way to think about what and how to name your child.

Lists are so powerful, I think, because they can be funny as well as insightful, instructive yet in the least bossy possible way. And when you've got a thousand different tactics to choose from, as you do here, you can adopt the ones that speak to you and ignore the rest.

Make no mistake: what's here is real help. Help of the practical, doable, manageable variety, with tangible payoffs. Some of these lists give you a more effective way to think or feel about an issue, some offer a quicker or easier or gentler route to achieving a goal, others show you how to fake it or advise you when the smartest solution is to do or say nothing at all. Some of this advice is designed to dispel guilt or doubt, some to promote confidence or imagination, and some just to give you a kick in the butt.

The result? A you that's still you, only a tiny bit sexier, smarter, richer, sweeter, thinner, and more together. But a whole hell of a lot happier.

SECTION ONE

79 WAYS

TO LOSE TWO POUNDS by Next Summer

6 Painless Ways to Cut 100 Calories a Day (and Lose a Pound a Month)

5 Ways to Choose a Diet and Exercise Plan You'll Stick With

11 Ways to Improve Your Mood (without Chocolate or Potato Chips)

7 Ways to Feel Thinner (Even If You're Not)

5 Tricks to Get Yourself to Eat Less

12 Foods to Have on Hand When You Start a Diet

12 Foods to Get Rid of before They Tempt You

The 1 Greatest Diet

6 Exercises for Confirmed Couch Potatoes

14 Ways to Stop Obsessing about Your Weight

PAINLESS WAYS TO CUT 100

CALORIES

A DAY

(AND LOSE A POUND A MONTH)

1. **Drink** your coffee black.

2. **Switch** one soft drink to diet, or one juice to water.

3. Eat the potatoes, but **skip the butter.**

4. Take your **dressing on the side**—or **squeeze** a lemon over your salad.

5. Use one piece of bread **instead** of two on your sandwich.

6. **Develop a taste** for mustard instead of mayonnaise, turkey instead of ham and cheese.

5 WAYS TO CHOOSE A DIET AND EXERCISE

PLAN YOU'LL **STICK WITH**

1. **BE REALISTIC.** Aiming to work out half an hour five days a week and eliminate bread from your diet is realistic; saying you'll get to the gym every day for two hours and go vegan overnight is not.

2. **KNOW THYSELF.** Like solo activities and resist authority? Then walk or opt for an elliptical machine over a yoga class. Love cookies and hate salads? Then pick a diet that allows for treats and lets you eat low-calorie food other than greens.

3. **MAKE IT EASY.** Schedule exercise and food prep at convenient times and places and you'll be most likely to stick to them.

4. **MAKE IT EFFICIENT.** Consistency of exercise is more important than duration; putting together salads from a salad bar and buying prepared foods can be just as healthful as time-consuming chopping and cooking.

5. **SET APPROPRIATE GOALS.** Breaking your goals into short-term achievable segments—bumping up your weights one notch and losing a maximum of two pounds—will keep you focused and motivated.

11

WAYS TO
IMPROVE

YOUR
MOOD

*(WITHOUT
CHOCOLATE OR
POTATO CHIPS)*

1. **Walk fast** around the block.

2. Put on a favorite white blouse or scarf—not the kind of thing you want to dribble crumbs on!

3. Call **someone you love** on a phone far from the kitchen.

4. Take a shower, bath, sauna, or swim— it's **restorative,** plus you can't eat while doing it.

5. **Go buy** yourself **something** (not food!). Oh, go on.

6. Go **scope out** what you're going to buy yourself when you lose ten pounds/save a hundred dollars/get your tax refund/pay off your credit cards. You can't eat in stores!

7. Indulge in a fashion magazine— **inspiration!**

8. **Plant** a flower, or pick one.

9. **Donate those cookies**—and some time and money along with them—to a local soup kitchen.

10. Construct a **fabulous** cookie-free salad for dinner.

11. Invite a similarly **weight-conscious friend** over for tea—and serve only that.

WAYS TO **FEEL**
THINNER
(EVEN IF YOU'RE NOT)

1. Cut **all the sizes** out of your clothes.

2. **Double** your **water intake** (to flush away the bloat).

3. Wear looser clothes (though wearing more figure-hugging ones will make you *look* **slimmer**).

4. Pull your shoulders back and your **tummy in**.

5. Invest in a **supportive, uplifting bra**.

6. Wear shoes with a bit of heel, a bit of **style**, a point to the toe.

7. Expose your **slimmest**, most attractive feature—wrist, ankle, neckline—and **hide** whatever makes you feel fat.

5

TRICKS

TO GET YOURSELF **TO EAT LESS**

1. Whenever you want to eat something, drink a glass of water first.

2. Serve your food in the kitchen rather than putting it on easily accessible platters on the table.

3. Use smaller plates.

4. For snacks, use really tiny plates, like cooks' prep plates, to hold the prescribed amount—15 almonds, say—of whatever you're eating.

5. When you're hungry, wait 15 minutes. Chances are the hunger will pass.

12

FOODS

TO HAVE ON HAND
WHEN YOU START **A DIET**

1. Herbs.

2. Berries.

3. Lemons and limes.

4. Sparkling water.

5. Sorbet.

6. Sliced turkey.

7. Shrimp.

8. Salsa.

9. Carrot sticks and peppers.

10. Mixed greens.

11. Herbal tea.

12. The best vinegar you can find.

12

FOODS

TO GET RID OF
BEFORE THEY **TEMPT YOU**

1. Cookies.

2. Potato chips.

3. White bread.

4. Steak.

5. Margarita and daiquiri mix.

6. And **the booze** that goes in it!

7. Brownie fixings.

8. Nuts.

9. Ice cream.

10. Bagels.

11. Lasagna.

12. The phone number of your favorite pizza
    and burrito delivery places.

THE

1

GREATEST

DIET

Lean protein, vegetables, and fruit. Period.

---

6 EXERCISES

FOR CONFIRMED **COUCH POTATOES**

1. **Walking.** Walking two miles burns nearly as many calories as running two miles—it just takes longer.

2. **Lifting** light weights.

3. Gentle **yoga**.

4. **Swimming**.

5. **Recumbent bicycling.** Come on, how hard can it be when its name includes the word *recumbent*?

6. **Water aerobics**.

14

WAYS TO STOP
OBSESSING
ABOUT
YOUR WEIGHT

1. **Volunteer** at a food-oriented charity: a soup kitchen, a food pantry.

2. Volunteer at a non-food-oriented **charity** helping people with problems **bigger than weight:** a kids' cancer ward, for instance, or a hospice.

3. **Donate** your scale and all your diet books to Goodwill.

4. Try on every single piece of clothing in your wardrobe and **get rid of everything** that doesn't fit and look good *right this very minute*.

5. Plant an **organic vegetable** garden—hard exercise and more healthful food, all in one.

6. Find a man who **worships** your body just the way it is.

7. Forget the picture of Kate Moss: put an attractive picture of **you** on the refrigerator.

8. Hire a professional to take a **gorgeous naked** picture of you.

9. Get rid of all magazines that make you feel less than **wonderful** about your body.

10. If your weight was perfect, what other problems would you still have? Make a list and set about **solving** those.

11. Make a list of all the things that are good about your weight: you get to eat cookies with impunity, for instance, or you have an awesome collection of size 14 s. Emphasize the **positive**.

12. If there are no positives and your weight is truly your biggest problem and you can't stop obsessing about how miserable you are, then you need to finally and truly commit to the kind of total life change that helps you take off the weight—and be willing to **embrace the pain** that goes along with that.

13. Know that most diets are unsuccessful, that even when you lose weight, 90 percent of the time you'll regain it, and that you may be wasting a lot of time and energy on an impossible **pursuit**.

14. Exercise for at least 20 minutes three times a week. Studies show that women who exercise feel better about their bodies **no matter what** they weigh.

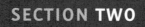

SECTION TWO

68 WAYS

TO ADD WEEKS to your life

12 Little Changes That Will Keep You Healthier This Year

11 Healthy Indulgences

9 Signs You're Too Stressed Out

7 Ways to Spend More Time in Dreamland

5 Good-for-You Snacks You Can Stick in Your Purse

10 Things That Get Better as You Get Older

8 Signs You Need a New Doctor

6 Times When Eating a Piece of Chocolate May Be the Healthiest Thing You Can Do

12

LITTLE CHANGES
THAT WILL KEEP
YOU
HEALTHIER
THIS YEAR

1. **Replace** your toothbrush.

2. Once in the morning and once in the evening, **walk around** the block.

3. Switch your beer or white wine for **red wine**.

4. Switch your soda, even if it's diet, for **water**.

5. Take your **salad dressing** on the side.

6. Wash your hands thoroughly and frequently.

7. If you work at a desk, **stretch** and walk around once every hour.

8. Wear your **seat belt**.

9. Wear **sunscreen**, even on nonsunny days.

10. Take a daily **multivitamin** made for women.

11. Switch your leather-soled shoes for rubber soles: better **traction**, kinder to your feet.

12. Don't talk on your **cell phone** when you drive. Talking on a cell phone causes a five-fold increase in accidents, according to one study, and is more dangerous than driving drunk.

11

HEALTHY

INDULGENCES

1. Shrimp.

2. Red wine.

3. Avocados.

4. Yoga.

5. Dark chocolate.

6. Almonds.

7. Laughter.

8. Sweet potatoes.

9. Berries.

10. Air-popped popcorn.

11. Naps.

9

SIGNS

YOU'RE TOO **STRESSED OUT**

1. You're up, showered, and dressed before you **realize** that blackness outside your window means it's actually the middle of the night.

2. You answer your home phone with your company name.

3. You can't figure out why your new car broke down, till the AAA guy tells you that you **ran out of gas**.

4. You don't realize you're **still eating** until you're on cookie #14.

5. You accidentally forwarded your instructions for the nanny to all your coworkers.

6. When a friend asks what you did last weekend or whether you've had lunch, you have **no idea**.

7. You go through the entire day before you realize you're wearing **two different shoes**.

8. You've rescheduled your **sex date** with your husband three times.

9. Your **fantasies** of escaping to a remote island have escalated to the point where you've decided what your new name will be.

7

WAYS TO SPEND MORE
TIME IN

DREAMLAND

1. **CLEAR YOUR BEDROOM.** Keeping your sleeping place clear of anything disturbing or distracting—messes, television, your computer, wiggling kids—can help you sleep better.

2. **ESTABLISH A BEDTIME ROUTINE THAT HELPS YOU UNHOOK FROM STRESS.** Build a destressing routine into the end of your day: take a warm bath, read a relaxing book, snuggle.

3. **DON'T DRINK.** Alcohol can help you fall asleep more quickly but tends to make you wake up in the middle of the night.

4. **COOL DOWN.** Crack a window or close the heating vents to keep your bedroom cooler, which aids sleep.

5. **STAY UP LATER.** If you fall into bed exhausted before 9 only to wake up at 3 and not fall asleep again until dawn, only to drag yourself through another day, the answer might be to adjust your bedtime later. You may find that if you go to bed at midnight, you sleep through the night and wake up refreshed.

6. **STOP THE SNORING.** Not your own, in all probability, but your spouse's. Some techniques: put an extra pillow under his head, get him to change his sleep position, use a steam vaporizer, look into nasal strips, or encourage him to lose weight!

7. **DON'T RUMINATE.** You wake up in the middle of the night. And then you lie there, thinking of everything that went wrong yesterday and will go wrong tomorrow. First, know that such dire ruminations are partly a brain trick: in the middle of the night, your brain produces a chemical that really does make everything look darker. Second, you can train yourself to unhook from middle-of-the-night obsessions by dwelling instead on pleasant memories and fantasies such as trying to remember all your childhood birthdays or your favorite fairy tales, or counting backwards slowly from 100, picturing each number as a golden figure fading into a black ground.

5

GOOD-FOR-YOU

SNACKS

**YOU CAN
STICK IN
YOUR PURSE**

1. A shiny hard apple
   (softer types tend
   to get bruised).

2. An energy bar.

3. Cheese sticks.

4. Almonds.

5. Carrots.

10

THINGS THAT GET

BETTER

AS YOU GET OLDER

1. Sex drive (yours, but
   alas, not his).

2. Friendships.

3. Long-held skills.

4. Vocabulary.

5. Eating habits.

6. Sense of diplomacy.

7. Expert knowledge.

8. Empathetic abilities.

9. Ability to separate what's
   important from
   what's not.

10. Control over such
    emotions as anger and
    impatience.

SIGNS **YOU NEED**
A NEW
DOCTOR

1. The receptionist is so cranky you put off calling for an appointment.

2. You wait for an hour or more to see the doctor, and then feel rushed when you finally make it to the **inner sanctum.**

3. The doctor or staff treats questions as intrusions.

4. The doctor or staff answers questions with some variation on, **"You don't need to know."**

5. Calling the office swamps you in a sea of voice mail options, none of which leads to a **live voice.**

6. Although you've visited several times, the doctor and staff have **no memory** of who **you** are.

7. The doctor and staff seem to change each time you visit.

8. You can't articulate why, but the doctor makes you **uncomfortable.**

6

TIMES WHEN **EATING**
A PIECE OF
CHOCOLATE
MAY BE THE HEALTHIEST
THING YOU CAN DO

1. When everyone else at the family party has started flinging the mashed potatoes.

2. When your husband has just informed you that he's sleeping with the babysitter—and he's not going to stop.

3. When the alternative is a **fluffer nutter** triple scoop sundae with extra fat.

4. When the alternative is **a cigarette**.

5. When you're training for a **marathon** and finding it difficult to keep weight on.

6. When you've been up with the baby and **chocolate** feels like your **only remaining pleasure**.

SECTION THREE

93 WAYS

TO BE SOMEWHAT SANER (or a Little Less Crazy)

11 Things Women Could Learn from Men

8 Times You Shouldn't Apologize No Matter How Badly You May Want To

9 Habits Worth Forming

9 Ways to Perk Up Your Mood Right This Minute

5 Ways to Build Your Confidence

10 Techniques for Minimizing Stress and Maximizing Holiday Pleasure

5 Resolutions You Just Might Keep

8 Pieces of Music Guaranteed to Calm You Down

11 DVDs Guaranteed to Cheer You Up No Matter How Bad Your Problem

12 Lines You Shouldn't Even Think About Crossing

5 Inspirational Quotes

11

THINGS

WOMEN

COULD LEARN

FROM

MEN

1. How to walk away from a dirty kitchen.

2. When it's business, not personal.

3. How to look in the mirror and, despite the extra 15 pounds, the egg on your shirt, and the $10 haircut, think you look fantastic.

4. When it's better just not to talk about it.

5. How to take out your anxiety on a football.

6. Why it's not your job to make everybody else happy.

7. How to believe you can drive a stickshift, build a shed, climb a mountain, or start a business, even if you've never tried it before.

8. How to believe the horoscope only when it's good.

9. Why it's okay to be friends and competitors at the same time.

10. How to forget a birthday and trust they'll love you anyway.

11. When it's just about sex, and why that might be okay.

8

TIMES YOU SHOULDN'T
APOLOGIZE
NO MATTER HOW BADLY
YOU MAY WANT TO

1. When someone bumps into you.

2. When you have to cancel because of serious illness or a death in the family.

3. When you can't read someone's mind.

4. When the plane is delayed, and you're not the pilot.

5. When you're dumping the guy who cheated on you.

6. When you and your friend both went on the diet, but only you lost weight.

7. When you and your friend both liked the guy, but he chose you.

8. When they try to make you feel like it's your fault . . . and you know it's not.

9

HABITS

WORTH FORMING

1. Flossing.

2. Getting to **the gym** on a regular schedule.

3. **Scheduling** your next teeth cleaning, Pap smear, and mammogram as soon as you complete your last one.

4. Clearing the kitchen counters **before** you go to bed.

5. **Making up** before you go to sleep.

6. Eating only one cookie.

7. Taking the stairs instead of the elevator.

8. Saying **thank you**.

9. Writing all your dates on one calendar.

9

WAYS TO **PERK UP**

YOUR MOOD

RIGHT THIS MINUTE

1. Before 5 P.M., grab any drink with maximum caffeine.

2. After 5 P.M., martini time!

3. Tell a five-year-old a knock-knock joke.

4. Listen to "Girls Just Want To Have Fun."

5. Put on something pink, yellow, or red.

6. Smile. It helps!

7. Buy yourself a bouquet of flowers.

8. Do jumping jacks.

9. Do something kind for someone, anyone—bring your elderly neighbor's paper to the door, give a homeless person a quarter.

5

WAYS TO **BUILD YOUR**

CONFIDENCE

1. Write down five accomplishments you're **proud of** and post the list in a place (the bathroom mirror! on your refrigerator!) where you'll see it often.

2. Ask a close friend to tell you all the reasons she thinks you're terrific—and offer to do the same for her in return.

3. Take a public speaking class: You'll pick up tips that will boost your confidence in other arenas.

4. Set a manageable **short-term goal**—to run a mile, to read one of the classic books—and make sure you meet it.

5. Psych yourself up by taking a short daily walk during which you chant some personal affirmations: I make a fantastic lasagna! I've got an inspiring laugh! My friends **love me!**

10

TECHNIQUES **FOR MINIMIZING STRESS AND MAXIMIZING**

HOLIDAY

PLEASURE

1. **Alternate** holiday activities with days you **pretend** it's not happening.

2. Order gifts for out-of-town friends and family online and have them wrapped and shipped **directly** to the recipient.

3. Limit kids' gifts to three, as in the **Three Wise Men**.

4. If you usually exchange individual gifts with siblings, friends, and/or coworkers, suggest you go to a Secret Santa system and **focus** on only one person each.

5. Beware of catching **too much** holiday spirit and over-commiting to activities. If you host a neighborhood cookie party, prepare an elaborate holiday meal for your extended family, help out a local charity, and plan a skiing holiday, you'll end up exhausted and broke and not having much fun at all.

6. Give to others, but don't forget to take care of **yourself**. It's okay to buy that perfect cashmere scarf you find on sale while you're gift-shopping or to schedule a massage as a break from holiday chores.

7. Buy different varieties of the same gift for everyone on your list: pajamas, umbrellas, board games.

8. Start **traditions** that focus more on pleasure than on work. Let your kids create holiday cards, treat your best friend to a lavish lunch rather than going crazy trying to find the perfect gift, ditch your annual jamboree for a quiet weekend at home with your spouse.

9. If you can, schedule a **getaway right before** Christmas: beat the crowds *and* the high prices.

10. Build in some fun for after the holiday: host a regifting party, reserve a January dinner at a nice restaurant, or plan your **summer vacation!**

5

RESOLUTIONS

YOU JUST **MIGHT KEEP**

Instead of: I'm going to lose 20 pounds.

TRY: Whenever I can, I'm going to choose to eat healthful food instead of crap.

Instead of: I'll go to the gym for two hours every single day.

TRY: For half an hour five days a week, I'll do something, even if it's just dance around my living room.

Instead of: This year, I will finally write that novel/paint that masterpiece/move to France.

TRY: This month, I will sign up for a class in writing/painting/French.

Instead of: I'm going to stop spending money on clothes and restaurants.

TRY: I'll make a budget for clothes and restaurant spending and I'll stay within that.

Instead of: I will hereafter never ever lose my temper with my family.

TRY: Before I lose my temper, I will take a deep breath, count to 100, and leave the room for at least three minutes. And then if I'm still mad, I'm going to let it rip!

8

PIECES OF **MUSIC GUARANTEED TO**

CALM YOU DOWN

1. Chanticleer, *And On Earth, Peace*

2. Chet Biscardi, *The Gift of Life*

3. Joan Baez, *Forever Young*

4. Henryk Gorecki, *Third Symphony*

5. Aaron Copland, *Appalachian Spring*

6. Samuel Barber, *Adagio for Strings*

7. Smokey Robinson, *Cruisin'*

8. Sufjan Stevens, *Come On! Feel the Illinoise!*

11

DVDS **GUARANTEED TO**

CHEER YOU UP

NO MATTER **HOW BAD YOUR PROBLEM**

1. **The 40-Year-Old Virgin:** When you're feeling like a loser at love.

2. **Arrested Development:** When it seems your family is hopelessly screwed up.

3. **Blades of Glory:** When a creative partnership goes awry.

4. **The Devil Wears Prada:** When your boss is driving you crazy.

5. **Harold and Maude:** When you feel too young or too old.

6. **As Good As It Gets:** When you think you're never going to find anybody.

7. **Annie Hall:** When you can't live with him, can't live without him.

8. **Bridget Jones's Diary:** When you've gained a few pounds.

9. **Some Like It Hot:** When you want to trade in your identity.

10. **Little Miss Sunshine:** When you want to stop trying.

11. **Dr. Strangelove:** When you're afraid the world is going to blow up.

12

LINES YOU **SHOULDN'T EVEN THINK ABOUT**

CROSSING

1. Cursing at work.

2. Sleeping with your boss, your next-door neighbor, your best friend's ex, or your ex's brother.

3. Telling a friend's secret.

4. Losing it with a customer service person or insurance rep – just feign an emergency, hang up, and call back.

5. Screaming at the waitress.

6. Dipping into your home equity for anything less than a life-saving operation.

7. Writing a check you know you can't cover.

8. Driving when you're only a little bit drunk.

9. Forgoing underwear in public.

10. Making racist or sexist jokes.

11. Criticizing someone for their religious or political beliefs.

12. Criticizing your spouse when other people are around.

5

INSPIRATIONAL
QUOTES

"Energy creates energy. It is by spending oneself that one becomes rich."

—Sarah Bernhardt

"I don't wait for moods. You accomplish nothing if you do that. Your mind must know it has to get down to work."

—Pearl Buck

"Be careful what you set your heart on, for it will surely be yours."

—Ralph Waldo Emerson

"Success is the ability to go from failure to failure without losing your enthusiasm."

—Winston Churchill

"Always dream and shoot higher than you know how to. Don't bother just to be better than your contemporaries or predecessors. Try to be better than yourself."

—William Faulkner

SECTION FOUR

92 WAYS

TO BE A SLIGHTLY KINDER FRIEND, SISTER, AUNT, NEIGHBOR, GUEST, and Even Total Stranger

6 Ways to Apologize Gracefully

14 Gentle Ways to Say No

7 Ways to Talk to Anybody's Mother

17 Things You Can't Say Too Often to the People You Love

7 Great Opening Lines That Work with Just About Anybody

7 Great Getaway Lines

10 Little Gifts to Thrill Any Little Girl

5 Original Hostess Gifts

8 Times You Don't Need to Feel Guilty about Being a Bitch

11 Times to Just Say Nothing

6

WAYS TO APOLOGIZE
GRACEFULLY

1. **The long way:** write an effusive, undefensive letter.

2. **The short way:** call immediately and say it was all your fault.

3. **The sweet way:** send white roses, expensive candy, or—in extreme cases—both.

4. **The funny way:** send a silly card, a strip-o-gram, or a video of you beating yourself.

5. **The longer way:** wait until both of you have forgotten what happened and then call to reconnect.

6. **The man's way:** pretend nothing happened.

14

GENTLE WAYS TO
SAY NO

1. I'm going to have to pass.

2. I'd love to, but I just don't have the time.

3. I made a resolution to start saying no more often.

4. I don't want to **say yes** and then let you down.

5. I'd love to, but my husband/kids/boss would freak out if I took on anything else.

6. Not right now.

7. Not this year.

8. You caught me at a terrible moment.

9. I can't say yes.

10. I don't want to say no, but I have to.

11. I'm just not **comfortable** with that.

12. It's just not right for me.

13. Ask me another time.

14. Please cross me off your list.

7

WAYS TO TALK TO ANYBODY'S
MOTHER

1. Ask what it was like for girls when she was in high school.

2. Ask for parenting **advice**.

3. Ask what she'd do differently if she was 21 again.

4. Commiserate about the ridiculousness of rap music, vegan diets, or thong underwear.

5. Offer to get her another **dessert**.

6. Ask if she's seen any good TV shows lately.

7. **Act shocked** that she has a child as old as she does.

1. I love you.

2. I understand.

3. Tell me more.

4. Poor baby.

5. I miss you.

6. I bought you a present.

7. Why don't you relax and let me handle it.

8. If you want to do it yourself, I'll help you.

9. I'm sorry.

10. Let's try again.

11. Let me give you a hug.

12. You're the best.

13. You look great.

14. Want some pie?

15. I'm sure it's going to work out all right.

16. Don't worry, we'll find the money.

17. I can't wait to see you again.

17

THINGS YOU
CAN'T SAY
**TOO OFTEN
TO THE
PEOPLE**

YOU
LOVE

7

GREAT OPENING
LINES
THAT WORK
WITH JUST
ABOUT ANYBODY

1. Hello.

2. What brings you here tonight?

3. You look like the most interesting person in the room.

4. Have you tried the shrimp/martini/birthday cake?

5. How did you **meet** the host/hostess?

6. Love your shirt.

7. Haven't we met somewhere before? **No, really.**

7

GREAT
GETAWAY LINES

1. Can you point me toward the powder room?

2. I have to say hello to the hostess.

3. I'm going to make my way over to the bar/the food/some other person.

4. So, who else should I meet?

5. Ooops, I've got to go sit down/stand up/get some air.

6. It's been **lovely** talking to you.

7. Excuse me.

10

LITTLE GIFTS **TO THRILL ANY**

LITTLE GIRL

1. Webkinz

2. Beanie babies

3. Candy

4. Crafts supplies

5. Stickers

6. Hair ornaments

7. Book gift cards

8. Mood rings

9. Thrift-store dress-up clothes

10. Money!

5

ORIGINAL **HOSTESS**

GIFTS

1. Instead of flowers, a flowering plant in a pretty pot.

2. Instead of a bottle of wine, a **special** vinegar or malt scotch.

3. Instead of a bakery cake, homemade cookies.

4. Instead of after-dinner chocolates, exotic decaf coffee.

5. Instead of soap or hand cream, vintage guest towels.

8

TIMES YOU DON'T NEED **TO FEEL GUILTY ABOUT BEING A**

BITCH

1. When he thinks "no" means "push harder."

2. When the friend you helped out—with an introduction, a recommendation, a loan—won't pay you back.

3. When you find someone's **unwelcome** hand on your butt.

4. When they promise to call and don't. Again.

5. When you've been nice, reasonable, assertive, and angry— and none of it has worked.

6. When someone reeking of liquor asks for a handout.

7. When you find out he saw her. Again.

8. When he **accuses** you of being one.

1. When the crazy guy on the train is trying to talk to you.

2. When they ask for volunteers to organize the neighborhood bake sale.

3. When your best friend asks whether that dress makes her look fat.

4. When the cop is giving you a **lecture** instead of writing you a ticket.

5. When there's two minutes left in the game, his team is six points down, they have the ball, and the clock is running.

11

TIMES **TO JUST SAY**
NOTHING

6. When you have the urge to tell someone about the really weird dream you had last night.

7. When someone you admire is giving you advice.

8. When you're fighting, and it's **his turn** to rant.

9. When the interviewer asks you why you left your last job, and the real reason is that you thought your boss was a jerk.

10. When you hate the food, but love the hostess.

11. When you're tempted to tell him about that **threesome** in Mexico.

SECTION FIVE

103 WAYS

TO HAVE A SLIGHTLY Better Relationship

8 Ways to Let Him Know You're Interested without Totally Embarrassing Yourself

6 Things You Can Tell about a Man before You Even Talk to Him

4 Productive Things to Do with New-Love Heat (When Your New Love's Not Around)

7 Kind Ways to Say No to a Second Date

9 Reasons to Be Happy You Still Aren't Married

9 Reasons to Be Happy You Still *Are* Married

8 No-Sweat Ways to Make Your Lover Feel Loved

11 Things It's Okay To Yada Yada

5 Questions to Ask Your Man before You Marry Him

6 Ways to Disagree (without Starting a Fight)

9 Ways to Make Up (without Giving In)

12 Times Not to Talk About It

9 Signs You Should Just Give Up

8

WAYS TO LET HIM **KNOW YOU'RE**
INTERESTED
WITHOUT TOTALLY EMBARRASSING YOURSELF

1. Throw a **party so big** it would be rude not to include him.

2. Send him a funny ecard, and be sure your return email address is in plain sight.

3. Make him a mix tape that's part fun, part soulful, part sexy.

4. Stalk him just enough to figure out which train he takes to work/where he buys his morning coffee/when he goes to the gym, and then happen to show up there.

5. Talk to one of **his friends.** For more on how this works, read the story of John Smith and Pocahontas, *Cyrano de Bergerac*, or watch Steve Martin and Daryl Hannah in *Roxanne*.

6. Call or email him for **advice on** something only he finds fascinating.

7. Position yourself close enough for **a kiss** on New Year's, and make it unforgettable.

8. Join his club, take up his hobby, root for his team—but please, not all three.

6

THINGS YOU CAN
TELL ABOUT A

MAN

BEFORE YOU EVEN
TALK TO HIM

1. How nervous you make him.

2. Whether he'll look you in the eye.

3. How much he cares about his clothes.

4. Whether his mother taught him to stand up straight.

5. How cool he wants you to think he is.

6. Whether he's willing to make the first move.

4

PRODUCTIVE
THINGS TO DO
WITH NEW-LOVE

HEAT

(WHEN YOUR
NEW LOVE'S
NOT AROUND)

1. Write a love song.

2. Train for a marathon.

3. Give your bedroom a top-to-bottom cleaning.

4. Shower some of that love on people who need it: a group of underachieving teenagers, kids at an inner-city daycare center.

7

KIND WAYS **TO SAY NO TO A**

SECOND DATE

1. My old boyfriend just came back into my life.

2. I'm moving and I'll get in touch when I'm settled.
   (Note: Won't work if the guy's your neighbor.)

3. I'm leaving on a long trip and I'll get in touch when I return.

4. I'd love to, but I just don't have time.

5. Would you help me take my mom to the hospital/take my cat to the vet/rototill my garden? (If he says yes to any of the above, reconsider! He might be worth a second—and third and fourth—date.)

6. I'm having too many problems right now to get involved.
   (For all he knows, your problems might be a broken nail.)

7. Sure, as long as you understand I'm never going to have sex with you.

1. Just when your career's hitting its stride, you have time to keep up with it.

2. You can **move to Paris,** become a vegan, or pursue a Chinese adoption without worrying about what anybody else **thinks**.

3. Pink sheets, pink towels, pink walls.

4. The place that you clean on Saturday is still clean on Sunday.

9

REASONS **TO BE HAPPY YOU STILL AREN'T** MARRIED

5. You still have **plenty of time** to plan your dream wedding.

6. Your ring finger is deliciously unfettered.

7. Meddling in-laws, stained boxers, discovering his porn cache on the computer—**not your problem!**

8. If you want, you never have to shave your legs, you can eat ice cream for dinner while watching *Beaches*, and you're free to spend all your **disposable** income on shoes.

9. Two dates in one day, a quickie with a near-stranger, and the possibility of meeting **Mr. Right** around the next corner are still in your future.

9

REASONS TO BE HAPPY YOU STILL ARE

MARRIED

1. No blind dates during which you **fantasize** about climbing out the ladies'-room window.

2. Always knowing what you're doing on Valentine's Day and your birthday.

3. Personal, in-house, full-time **bed-warmer.**

4. Burping? Farting? Coming down with the flu? He doesn't even blink.

5. He's met **your mother** and he didn't run the other way.

6. You can be pretty sure he's not gay, crazy, or married to someone else.

7. All those rough **patches**—Will he call? Should I say I love him? What if he dumps me at the altar?—are behind you.

8. If you **get pregnant** or lose your job, you know he'll be there for you.

9. He knows all the **secret** ways to turn you on in two seconds flat.

8

NO-SWEAT **WAYS TO** **MAKE YOUR LOVER**

FEEL LOVED

1. Buy a beautiful frame and fill it with that adorable childhood **picture** of him.

2. Cook him that thing he loves—the one with the 97 grams of fat.

3. Give him a **lap dance.**

4. Make out with him in the car, even if you're sitting in your own driveway.

5. Watch the game with him, and try to be **interested.**

6. Write him a **love letter,** douse it with perfume, and send it through the mail.

7. When he's had a rough week, cancel the Friday night dinner party.

8. For once, you sleep on the **wet spot.**

11

THINGS IT'S
OKAY **TO**

YADA
YADA

1. The details of all your other relationships (but not the fact that you had them).

2. What happened between the time you pulled out of the driveway and brought the car home with a **dent** in the rear door.

3. Your complete urinary tract infection history.

4. What colleague #1 said after colleague #2 told her that your boss said that. . .

5. How exactly it was that you got George Clooney's home telephone number.

6. Every course you ever took in college.

7. Everything that went through your mind when you met your old **boyfriend** in the street.

8. All the time spent in the bathroom.

9. How much you paid for those shoes.

10. What you thought about him before you decided you liked him.

11. What you and your old **roommates** talk about on your annual spa weekend.

5

QUESTIONS TO **ASK YOUR MAN**
BEFORE YOU
MARRY HIM

1. Do you want to have children, and if so, how many and when?

2. What are your **expectations** for sharing breadwinning and housework?

3. How do you feel about my **family**?

4. What would make you want to get divorced?

5. What's your **ideal** of our marriage in five years, ten, twenty, fifty?

6

WAYS **TO**

DISAGREE

(WITHOUT STARTING A FIGHT)

1. I'd love to hear more about why you feel that way.

2. That's a really different **perspective** from any I would have thought of.

3. It would never occur to me to look at it that way.

4. How about if we do it your way this time and mine the next.

5. How about if we do it my way **this time** and yours the next.

6. Let's find another alternative we're both enthusiastic about.

1. Bake him a pie.

2. Wear **high heels**. And no panties.

3. Rent any one of the following
   make-up-without-giving-in movies:

   Something's Gotta Give
   Mr. & Mrs. Smith
   Intolerable Cruelty
   The Awful Truth
   10 Things I Hate About You

WAYS **TO**

MAKE UP
(WITHOUT GIVING IN)

4. Tell him you're going to allow him to kiss your feet
   (which he may not do—but at least you'll make him laugh).

5. Make him **laugh**.

6. Make reservations at his favorite restaurant.

7. Invite his mother over (and be really nice to her).

8. Have sex with him.

9. If you can't talk or have sex, put your arms around him in
   the middle of the night and hold on until neither of you
   are mad anymore.

12

TIMES NOT
TO **TALK**

ABOUT IT

1. When you know the thing you want to say ("You're just like your father!") is sure to make him furious.

2. When you've **noticed** a little more hair in the sink. . . and a little less on his head.

3. When your friends think he's a jerk, but telling him is only going to make him hate your friends.

4. When all you want to do is **criticize**. Really.

5. When he's doing anything with power tools.

6. When the only thing you can think to say is a **lie**.

7. When you'd really rather have sex.

8. In the final two minutes of any game.

9. When he's just had a fight with his mother.

10. When you're **tempted to confess** some ancient sin that's already been atoned for.

11. When you've just achieved some wonderful new level—made love for the first time, decided to get married—and you should just let yourself enjoy it for a moment before moving on to the next issue.

12. When you can tell that even if you were Scarlett Johanssen, and you were naked, and you were telling him you thought he was the most **fascinating** man in the world, he wouldn't be in the mood to listen.

SIGNS YOU **SHOULD JUST**
GIVE UP

1. You realize you like him a lot better when you're not with him.

2. You start telling yourself maybe you're just one of those women who doesn't enjoy sex.

3. You find all kinds of things you absolutely positively have to do—scrub the grout in the shower tile, read last Sunday's sports section—instead of going to bed with him.

4. You dread Valentine's Day.

5. You turn the TV on as soon as he walks in the room.

6. You've tried therapy...and things got worse.

7. You find yourself browsing match.com.

8. You get undressed in the dark. In your closet.

9. All your daydreams are of how great life would be, if only you were alone.

SECTION SIX

95 WAYS

TO BE A SEXUAL Demigoddess

7 **Ways** to Feel Sexier in 5 Minutes or Less

9 **Things** Never to Say to a Naked Man

10 **Rules** for Slightly Better Kisses

12 **Effective Ways** to Get in the Mood (without Ruining Your Makeup)

13 **Ways** to Make Him Feel Like a Fabulous Lover

6 **Times** Imaginary Sex Is Hotter Than Real

11 **Signs** Your Sex Life Is Going Well

10 **Advantages** of Having a Longtime Lover

17 **Things** That Are Better Than Sex

7

WAYS TO FEEL
SEXIER
IN 5 MINUTES **OR LESS**

1. Put on a cleavage-boosting red lace bra.

2. Listen to Marvin Gaye's **"Let's Get It On."**

3. Remember that cute guy at the party who said to you in a sexy Southern or British (or even Brooklyn) accent, "I'm just crazy about you."

4. Put on some red lipstick.

5. Go commando.

6. Watch the scenes of *Closer* in which Clive Owens appears.

7. Imagine Clive Owens kissing the back of your neck.

9

THINGS NEVER
TO SAY TO A
NAKED
MAN

1. So, tell me all about your mother.

2. Are you **attracted to** (insert name of your best friend)?

3. Are you attracted to (insert name of *his* best friend)?

4. I **trust** this means **we're getting married.**

5. You don't mind if my cat gets on the bed, do you?

6. Wait right there while I get the whip and **the handcuffs.**

7. I've got this infection. (Then again, don't *not* say it.)

8. Yikes, do you need to get to the gym!

9. Is that it?

10

RULES FOR
**SLIGHTLY
BETTER**

KISSES

1. **MAKE SURE YOUR MOUTH IS FRESH AND CLEAN.** Of course, you don't want to smell like a mouthwash factory, but you don't want to reek of garlic either.

2. **MAKE A SUBTLE APPROACH.** You've seen it done in the movies: Edge closer. Stop talking. Turn your face to the side for nose clearance. Then, if all the signs say go, move in for the kiss.

3. **DON'T LICK YOUR LIPS PREKISS.** Yum yum? No no.

4. **FOCUS ON THE MOUTH.** Don't take a kiss as a license to move in with all other body parts.

5. **KISS ONE LIP AT A TIME.** Perfect opening gambit.

6. **OPEN YOUR MOUTH ONLY AS FAR AS YOUR PARTNER DOES.**

7. **INTRODUCE YOUR TONGUE GENTLY.** Think of it as a give and take, and make sure you're getting a response to your gives.

8. **BREATHE THROUGH YOUR NOSE.**

9. **GO FOR VARIETY.** Hard. Then soft. Tongue. Then no tongue. Gentle. Then passionate.

10. **WHEN IT'S OVER, IT'S OVER.** Don't try to keep kissing if your partner's lost interest.

12

EFFECTIVE WAYS TO GET

IN THE MOOD

(WITHOUT **RUINING YOUR MAKEUP**)

1. Send each other erotic emails.

2. Slow dance to Norah Jones' "Turn Me On."

3. Dirty dance to anything.

4. Dirty talk about anything.

5. Tell him what you'd like him to do, in French.

6. Ask him to help you shave your legs.

7. Feed each other strawberries.

8. Pretend you're 13 and kiss until you can't stand it anymore.

9. Take a long walk holding hands.

10. Watch a romantic movie with your arms around each other.

11. Tell him a secret.

12. Sleep first, have sex later.

13

WAYS TO
MAKE HIM
**FEEL LIKE A
FABULOUS**

LOVER

1. Surprise him with new lingerie.

2. Write him an **erotic** story.

3. Take naked pictures of him.

4. Call him for some **phone sex**—even if he's in the next room.

5. Wake him up in the middle of the night.

6. Take him sex toy shopping.

7. Ask him if he's ever starred in a porn film.

8. Kidnap him at work and take him to a hotel.

9. Next time you're out together, whisper that you'd love to take him into the bathroom for a **quickie**. Pray he doesn't take you up on it.

10. Play footsie under the table.

11. Send him a **love letter**—perfumed, of course.

12. Tell him all your fantasies about him.

13. Do it somewhere dangerous—in the woods, in the bathroom at a party, on the kitchen table with the curtains open in the middle of the afternoon.

6

TIMES IMAGINARY SEX IS

HOTTER

THAN **REAL**

1. When you're nine months pregnant or a brand-new mom.

2. When try as he might, he just can't **find the spot.**

3. When you just saw a Brad Pitt movie but your date is more Wallace Shawn.

4. When your partner is **battery-operated.**

5. When you're just waking up from a really hot dream.

6. When you're crazy about him but you haven't moved it into the **bedroom.**

1. Your friends keep asking why your skin looks so amazing.

2. Monogamy feels like the most natural thing in the world.

3. On the nights he just wants to **snuggle**, you're disappointed.

4. George Clooney? Phooey. You always fantasize about *him*.

5. You can't remember where you stashed your **vibrator**.

6. Or your pajamas.

7. You've lost ten pounds, and you're still eating ice cream.

8. You always sleep in each other's arms.

9. **Frequency?** Twice. A day.

10. Even when he's dressed, you keep picturing him **naked**.

11. Movies, toys, erotica—there's nothing you're not up for trying together.

11

SIGNS
YOUR

SEX
LIFE

IS **GOING WELL**

10

ADVANTAGES
**OF HAVING A
LONGTIME**
LOVER

1. No big between-the-sheets surprises—
   you want me to do *what?!?*

2. No awkward conversations about birth
   control or STDs.

3. He's pretty much made **peace** with
   your white cotton panties.

4. When he buys you lingerie for your birthday
   he gets the right size. But he also
   knows you're going to return it.

5. Whether you're in the mood for calming,
   loving, or rock-the-house sex, you know
   how to get it from him.

6. You can tell him all your fantasies, and
   maybe even act out a few.

7. He'll appreciate your body even when
   you don't suck in your stomach.

8. After sex, you can move directly to sleep
   or *The Colbert Report* without anyone's
   feelings getting hurt.

9. When you **sleep** together, you can
   actually *sleep*.

10. You don't have to wonder whether he
    loves you: you know he does.

1. The *anticipation* of sex with someone you're crazy about.

2. Slipping under **warm** covers on a cold night.

3. Saying **"I love you"** for the first time.

4. The first chocolate chip cookie at the end of a long, successful diet.

5. Those golden moments when you feel smart *and* beautiful.

17

THINGS
THAT ARE
BETTER
THAN
SEX

6. Rediscovering your **first** love.

7. Realizing you're totally over the guy who did you wrong.

8. Finding the perfect dress, in your size, marked half off.

9. **Skydiving**—and landing in one piece.

10. Doing the thing that terrifies you—giving the speech, meeting his parents—and feeling yourself move beyond your fear.

11. Taking the pregnancy test, and getting the result you hope for.

12. Going to Paris for the first time. And the second and third times, too.

13. The kind of **massage** that makes you so relaxed you drool.

14. Making up after a big fight.

15. Feeling the baby *finally* nod off in your arms.

16. Unwrapping the present and finding it's the thing you didn't even dare to want.

17. Wanting what you **already have**.

SECTION SEVEN

81 WAYS

TO LOOK MORE LIKE Angelina Jolie
(or At Least Less Like Your Aunt Ethel)

8 Easy Pieces for Effortless Style

9 Ways to Conquer the Mall in Under 56 Minutes

5 Pieces That Are a Waste of Money

1 Item Most Worth a Splurge

9 Things to Wear That Make You Look Thin (Even When You're Not)

8 Steps to Pain-Free Closet-Pruning

11 Items of Clothing That Really Are Timeless

7 Efficient Packing Strategies

8 Near-Instant Ways to Look Six Months Younger

5 Cures for a Bad Hair Day

10 Invisible Beauty Tricks

EASY PIECES FOR **EFFORTLESS**
STYLE

1. A leather jacket.

2. A scarf that costs as much as any other single item you wear.

3. Signature earrings or glasses (not, dear God, both) against a classic backdrop.

4. Neutrals mixed in unexpected ways: navy with black, brown with gray, white with ivory.

5. Textures mixed in equally unexpected ways: silk with tweed, cashmere with shiny lurex, denim with velvet.

6. Suede, jersey, lightweight wool knit—luxurious fabrics that don't wrinkle.

7. One bold, flattering color—periwinkle blue, magenta— that you wear in accents via a scarf or gloves or shoes with a maximum of two neutrals.

8. Two accessory focal points: earrings and bracelet, for example, or necklace and belt buckle.

1. **WEAR COMFORTABLE SLIP-ON (AND -OFF) SHOES AND MINIMAL, EASY-TO-REMOVE LAYERS.** You're dressing for quick touring and changing-room speed.

2. **SHOP FIRST THING IN THE MORNING ON A WEEKDAY.** Stores are emptiest, salespeople and merchandise freshest. Second choice: Dinner hour.

3. **SHOP ALONE.** No kids, girlfriends, or husbands.

4. **HEAD DIRECTLY TO THE SHOPS OR DEPARTMENTS YOU LIKE BEST.** Don't get distracted by the designer sale. Do not decide to buy running shoes or your niece's birthday gift, just because you're here.

WAYS TO
CONQUER THE

THE
MALL

IN UNDER
56 MINUTES

5. **TAKE A FAST TOUR OF THE AISLES.** If nothing looks good, move on.

6. **GRAB A SALESPERSON OR MAKE A SECOND, ITEM-GRABBING SWING THROUGH THE RACKS.** You're heading into the fitting room.

7. **IN THE FITTING ROOM, UNDRESS ONLY AS MUCH AS YOU HAVE TO.** You don't have to take off your shirt to figure out you can pull a skirt up over your knees.

8. **IF YOU WANT SOMETHING, HAND OVER YOUR CREDIT CARD IN THE FITTING ROOM.** Your pieces should be rung up and ready for you by the time you're dressed.

9. **IF NOTHING'S WORKING, MOVE ON.** Don't agonize, compromise, or try harder. Just motor to the next store.

5

PIECES THAT ARE A **WASTE OF**
MONEY

1. **CHEAP SILK, LINEN, OR CASHMERE THAT NEEDS TO BE DRYCLEANED.** These fabrics don't hold up to wear and the necessary cleaning will negate any price savings.

2. **SOMETHING TO WEAR TO A WEDDING.** Unless you're in the wedding party or find a perfect dress for $29.99, resist the urge to splurge on something that, like most wedding dresses, you'll wear only once.

3. **DEEPLY DISCOUNTED DESIGNER PIECES THAT DON'T WORK FOR YOUR WARDROBE, YOUR BODY, OR YOUR LIFESTYLE.** If you're a label slut, it can be difficult to resist Prada at 75 percent off. But if you wouldn't buy it at full price if you could afford to, then don't waste your money no matter how deep the discount.

4. **SOMETHING THAT WILL FIT YOU WHEN YOU LOSE TEN POUNDS.** Make sure you can return it or risk facing a piece that will forever taunt you with your lack of dieting success.

5. **SHOES THAT HURT, JUST A LITTLE BIT.** They'll stretch, says the salesman. They won't. They'll feel better once you break them in. Again, they won't. Unless you plan to wear them only to bed, skip this item.

ITEM MOST **WORTH A**

SPLURGE

Designer shoes that are both easy on the feet and class up anything you wear them with.

THINGS TO **WEAR THAT MAKE YOU LOOK**

THIN

(EVEN WHEN YOU'RE NOT)

1. Long lean black pants hemmed to just above the ground.

2. High heels.

3. A top that crosses over in front.

4. A long vee-neck cardigan.

5. A shirt or sweater with some shape at the waist and coverage at the hips.

6. Dark pinwale corduroys—almost always more flattering than jeans.

7. A wrap dress.

8. A shaped jacket with shoulder padding.

9. Underwear that smooths and fits well so that it doesn't create rolls and bumps.

STEPS TO **PAIN-FREE**

CLOSET-PRUNING

1. Start by taking everything out of your closet. **Yes, everything.**

2. Thoroughly **clean** all shelves, vacuum and mop floors, weed out wire hangers.

3. Next, put back **everything** you wear OFTEN, and that's also in good repair, fits, and is in season. Not including those items you spent a lot for but haven't worn much. Just the jeans you find your-self pulling on every day, the jacket you find yourself reaching for on every important occasion, the sexy boots you can walk three miles in.

4. If you're like most women (me, for instance), your closet will still be pretty bare. Your next step is to replace those items that fit, are right for the current season, and that you've worn at least three times in the past year.

5. You may still have more clothing outside the closet than in it. Now go to a **triage system.** In the first class are those items you're ready to give to charity: everything that never fit you right, or that makes you feel awful when you look at it. Stuff those items directly into a

giveaway bag. Consider donating work clothes you've moved beyond to a charity like Dress for Success (dressforsuccess.org), which supplies women with interview gear.

6. In the second group are those things that need to go into **seasonal storage.** Be sure to clean pieces before you store them: food and perspiration invite moths to feed, and invisible stains—from champagne, for instance, or a clear soda such as Sprite—turn brown over time if not removed. If there are items in this group you're torn about off loading, pack them away (assuming you have room) and reconsider when you take them out again, when any emotional attachment will have lessened.

7. The third group, which may be **sizeable**, contains those items you haven't worn in a long time, that don't fit quite right, or that don't work for your life. Because they were a great bargain, because they carry sentimental attachment, or because you simply and irrationally love them, you're loath to get rid of them. Rather than putting these items back in your closet or forcing yourself to throw them away, pack them into storage and **reconsider** in six months or a year. Chances are it will be either easy to get rid of them then—you can sell anything worth money on eBay—or reembrace the pieces you truly missed.

8. Great tip for **preserving** the memory of those pieces it's time to say goodbye to, but that you still love: **Take photographs** and store in your closet.

11

ITEMS OF CLOTHING **THAT REALLY ARE**

TIMELESS

1. An Hermès scarf.

2. A black cashmere turtleneck.

3. Diamond studs.

4. A straight, black knee-length skirt.

5. A black leather tote bag.

6. Red leather gloves.

7. A white shirt.

8. A tan belted trench coat.

9. Jeans, in a great fit and a nonfancy cut.

10. Black suede loafers.

11. A white tee shirt.

7

EFFICIENT **PACKING**
STRATEGIES

1. Lay clothes you're thinking of wearing on your bed before you pack, to make sure you have **everything you need**, everything matches, and you're not duplicating.

2. Focus on **two neutral** colors—tan and black, for instance—with a few bright accents to maximize mixing and matching.

3. Choose items that do double duty: a tee shirt you can wear to bed, jeans that can be dressed up or down, a pareo that works as a beach coverup or evening shawl.

4. **Think layering,** not bulk. Three thin cotton or silk pieces trump one chunky knit.

5. Minimize shoes, bras, dressy pieces, coats.

6. Pick lightweight nylon or lace underwear and socks that can be laundered easily and dry quickly.

7. Bring one item that may not be practical, but that always makes you feel great. Even if you just wear that **cashmere** turtleneck in your hotel room, the psychic comfort will be worthwhile.

NEAR-INSTANT **WAYS TO LOOK**
SIX MONTHS
YOUNGER

1. Cover the gray. Yes, there are women with gorgeous gray hair, and their name is Judy Collins. For the rest of us, coloring the gray subtracts six years, not six months.

2. Update or ditch your glasses.

3. Make your lipstick paler and your blush brighter.

4. Wear undergarments that do what your muscles used to.

5. Stand up straight!

6. Wrap a pale pink or pale blue scarf around that neck you feel bad about.

7. If you have long hair, wear it up. If you have short hair, wear it loose.

8. Whiten your teeth.

5

CURES FOR **A BAD**

HAIR DAY

1. A grooming cream that lets you restyle without rewashing.

2. A chignon.

3. A wide black or **tortoiseshell** headband.

4. A messy ponytail—hey, it's supposed to look that way!

5. A **hat**—straw, knit, your favorite team cap.

10

INVISIBLE

BEAUTY

TRICKS

1. Put on moisturizer with sunscreen while skin is damp.

2. Add a thin smudgy line of dark brown eyeliner to your top lids to **define eyes** in a **nonobvious** way.

3. More important than buying **expensive** mascara is to buy NEW mascara every three months, so it goes on creamier and doesn't clump.

4. Use the same cream blush in a rosy shade for a natural glow on cheeks AND lips.

5. If you use concealer under eyes or to camouflage spots, don't go too pale, and investigate rosy or yellowed shades to better match your skin.

6. Rather than **powder**, use **blotting paper** to keep down shininess on forehead, nose, chin.

7. To even out skin color or tone down **redness**, instead of lathering on powder or foundation, consider a dermatological redness concealer available either over the counter (Dermablend makes one) or by prescription.

8. For hair that's smooth without being flat, use conditioner first, THEN shampoo.

9. If you're coloring your hair or covering gray, go to an excellent colorist the first time around (ask your friends) and ask him or her to custom-mix you a color—and be sure to get **the formula** to take with you.

10. To add volume, shampoo before bedtime and sleep with your hair pulled into a **ponytail** on top of your head.

SECTION EIGHT

86 WAYS

TO BE A LESS Desperate Housewife

17 Things to Throw or Give Away Now

11 No-Sweat Habits for a Cleaner House

9 Ways to Get Your Husband to Do More

7 Ways to Make Your House Look Clean (without Actually Cleaning It)

7 Sneaky Home-Decorating Shortcuts

5 Guilt-Free Ways to Create a Room of Your Own

10 Steps to a Fabulous Party

5 Ways to Calm a Crying Baby

11 Ways Not to Yell at Your Kid (This Time)

4 Ways to Discipline Your Kids in Public without Making a Scene

THINGS TO **THROW OR**
GIVE AWAY NOW

1. Any white shirt that's yellowed under the arms.

2. Any **underwear** you wouldn't want to be in an accident in.

3. Any book that makes you feel guilty when you look at it.

4. Any package of flour, sugar, pasta, or anything that's been open for longer than three months.

5. Last year's **spices.**

6. Magazines you've read **twice.**

7. Clothes that make you feel bad about your body or your life.

8. Shoes that hurt.

9. Linens that you wouldn't want to have your nose buried in for eight hours.

10. Old mismatched towels you're keeping "in case." In case of what? Invasion by a horde of unclean relatives? You don't want to be **prepared** for that.

11. Those 28 tiny bottles of body lotion you swiped from hotels and have never gotten around to using.

12. The gifts you hated as soon as you opened them but have felt too guilty to get rid of.

13. The wrapping paper from said gifts.

14. Dried wreaths or bouquets that have become more dust than flower.

15. Any broken lamp or appliance that would cost more to fix than to replace.

16. Anything you use only occasionally—pliers, staple remover, apple corer—that you have more than one of.

17. Any photograph you don't want your grandchildren to remember you by.

11

NO-SWEAT
**HABITS FOR
A CLEANER**
HOUSE

1. Make your bed the minute you get out of it.

2. Sort your **mail** over the recycling bin as soon as you bring it in the house.

3. Always tidy up the biggest thing in the room first: clear the dining room table, make the bed, straighten the slipcover on the sofa.

4. Take off your **shoes** at the front door.

5. Hang up coats and put away hats and gloves as soon as you take them off.

6. After meals, have everyone clear their plates directly into the dishwasher.

7. **Put away clothes** before you get in bed.

8. Place a hamper near the **shower**.

9. Put a wastebasket in every room.

10. Clean out your refrigerator and pantry as you put away groceries.

11. Once a week, clear off every surface in each room into the center of the floor, where it's easiest to sort into **piles** to keep and trash.

9

WAYS TO GET **YOUR**
HUSBAND
TO DO **MORE**

1. Admire the total **superiority** of his stove-cleaning or window-washing technique.

2. Suggest tandem naked cleaning.

3. Tell him how much it **costs** to hire someone.

4. Tell him you're going to hire a 25-year-old named Jed. Who's straight.

5. Make it a **competition:** the one who gets more done wins the sexual favor of his choice. Let him win!

6. Ask him to do jobs you know he likes.

7. Enlist the help of **his mom** or his best buddy.

8. Divide chores evenly and let him choose which half of the list he wants.

9. If you need more tips, check out *The Lazy Husband: How to Get Men to Do More Parenting and Housework*, by Joshua Coleman, Ph.D.

7

WAYS TO MAKE **YOUR HOUSE**

LOOK CLEAN

(WITHOUT ACTUALLY **CLEANING IT**)

1. Clear off all surfaces into laundry baskets.

2. Stash laundry baskets in closets.

3. If it can't be cleared and stashed, stack it.

4. Windex the mirrors.

5. Shine the sinks and the faucets.

6. Spray cleaning product in kitchen and bathroom (doesn't have to actually be used to clean anything) and light a scented candle—the most expensive one you can afford—in the living room.

7. Dim the lights.

7

SNEAKY **HOME-DECORATING**

SHORTCUTS

INSTEAD OF:	CONSIDER:
Renovating your kitchen.	Replacing the countertops.
Painting the exterior of your house.	Painting your front door red.
Reupholstering the furniture.	Switching from overhead lights to lamps.
Buying new drapes.	Washing your windows and switching to sheers.
Redoing the bathroom.	Retiling the shower.
Replacing the carpeting.	Buying a great area rug.
Building new storage units.	Getting rid of your junk!

GUILT-FREE WAYS TO **CREATE**

A ROOM

OF YOUR **OWN**

1. **Choose a place where you can close the door, even if it's not a room dedicated entirely to you.** A corner of a guest room or even your bedroom can work; a piece of the kitchen is less desirable.

2. **Make the space your own.** If you have lots of books, import bookshelves. If you like to write while reclining, get yourself a chaise. The point is: Don't just make do with whatever is already there.

3. **Keep out distractions.** You might consider NOT installing a phone line or wireless Internet.

4. **Stay inspired.** You might want to put up a bulletin board on which you can tack ideas and other inspiring items, or paint a wall with chalkboard-type paint so you can write directly on it.

5. **Accommodate your family.** To keep kids occupied and help them understand what you're doing when you're in your own room, help them to create their own special place, complete with their writing materials, art supplies, etc.

10

STEPS TO A **FABULOUS**

PARTY

1. Send **invitations** by email, either via evite.com or your own cute missive. Skip the RSVPs; just count on 80% or so of the people you invite showing up.

2. **Don't bother cleaning** before the party—just clear off all surfaces and save your cleaning muscle for after the event.

3. Put more **energy** into the drinks than the food, creating a really fun signature cocktail—think Mojitos or Sidecars—and augmenting that with white wine, beer, and club soda. People will bring extra wine and supply you with red.

4. Do all your **shopping** in one power sweep of your local Costco or similar megamarket. Good bets: cooked shrimp, precut vegetables, guacamole and chips, grapes and cheese, cookies.

5. Go all out with a big bouquet of splashy flowers as a centerpiece. Bright paper garlands, twinkly fairy lights, and votive candles can also be festive.

6. Make an iPod party playlist or enough mix CDs to get you through the entire evening, including at least a half hour to elevate your energy and mood before guests arrive.

7. Set out all your food and drinks before the party begins. Your special cocktail should be in a pitcher, with backups in the fridge, with glasses nearby. Beer, wine, and soda should be in an ice-filled bucket. Place food and drinks at opposite ends of your house or apartment to encourage guests to move around.

8. Dim the lights.

9. Dress in something fabulous. Really fabulous. Indulge in your highest, sexiest heels—you don't have to walk anywhere, you're already home!

10. Have lots of fun. A relaxed hostess who's focused on her guests, not on the food or the drinks or picking up every last cocktail napkin, is the most important ingredient of a successful party.

5

WAYS TO **CALM A**
CRYING BABY

1. Sing "You Ain't Nothin' but a Hound Dog."

2. **Dance around** the living room.

3. Drive around the block—**two hundred times**.

4. Rub the baby's stomach.

5. Rub your stomach, pat your head, hop on one foot, and make a silly face.

WAYS NOT TO **YELL AT**

YOUR KID

(THIS **TIME**)

1. Turn up the radio (even if, maybe especially if, it's the rap station).

2. Go for **a walk** around the block.

3. Take said kid out for **ice cream**.

4. Take ten—**make that** 50—deep cleansing breaths, breathing in what you want (patience) and out what you don't (anger).

5. Think about what yelling's going to **accomplish** (in most cases, nothing positive) and how else you can get what you want (a discussion, a conference, a revised routine, discipline, bribery).

6. Think about how it felt when your mom yelled at you.

7. Think about your kid, 30 years from now, thinking about how it felt when you yelled at him.

8. Think about the **therapy bills**.

9. Give yourself **a time-out**.

10. Call a friend

11. **Hug** your child.

4

WAYS TO **DISCIPLINE**

YOUR KIDS

IN **PUBLIC WITHOUT MAKING A SCENE**

1. With a small child who's having a **meltdown**, pick her up, hold her tight, and carry her away.

2. With an older child, say, "We'll work this out at home, but for now, let's just get through this meal."

3. When neither reason nor discipline are working, **take a deep breath,** step back and wait a minute, and then try again.

4. If all else fails, **bribery** is usually effective!

SECTION NINE

73 WAYS

TO RAISE YOUR IQ by At Least Five Points

15 **Ways** to Remember What You Ate for Breakfast

11 **Things** You Can Learn in an Afternoon

15 **One-Sentence** Guides to Great Books

10 **Neurobic** Exercises

7 **Unfathomable Concepts,** Simplified

4 **Unpronounceable Names,** Clarified

5 **Easy Ways** to Keep Up with World Events

6 **Big Words** You Can Toss Around

WAYS TO **REMEMBER WHAT**

YOU ATE

FOR **BREAKFAST**

1. Rewrite information you need to remember or **repeat** it out loud.

2. Find new relationships to material you need to remember: If someone's street address is 23, for instance, recall that's the age of your assistant and the date of your anniversary.

3. Relate information to the **senses**: colors, tastes, textures, smells.

4. Use visual images to remember things—you might think of a cup of coffee to remember the name Joe, for example— and make them bold, vivid, colorful, and positive. A big, red, steaming, delicious cup of coffee!

5. Another technique for remembering names: Relate the person's name to something distinctive about their appearance.

6. To remember something like a **password**, construct a sentence with its first letters: hmsatt might translate to something like Her Man Sings Arias Totally Tunelessly.

7. Rhymes and jokes make things easier to remember: right is tight, for example.

8. If you take notes on a subject you need to remember, reorganize the notes later.

9. Drink more tea: a British study says drinking black and green tea improves memory via brain chemistry.

10. Break information down into smaller chunks. Instead of trying to commit an entire ten-digit phone number to memory, for example, remember it in three or four distinct pieces.

11. Associate each piece of a long string of information, such as the text of a speech or a long shopping list, with a place along a route you know well, such as your drive to work or the plot of a classic fairy tale.

12. Make up a story that links the items you need to remember.

13. Review and rehearse information soon after learning it and then at spaced intervals rather than cramming all at once and never revisiting the subject.

14. Practice, practice, practice. Instead of writing everything down, consciously make yourself remember the phone number of the restaurant, the address of the dentist, all the spices in the recipe.

15. Feel positive about your ability to remember. Saying you have a bad memory can actually make it more difficult to remember!

11

THINGS YOU **CAN**

LEARN

IN AN **AFTERNOON**

1. How to **navigate** the airport and hotel in Spanish.

2. How to bake a **pizza**.

3. The plots of all of Jane Austen's novels.

4. The basic elements of kitchen design.

5. How to knit a simple sweater.

6. How to take a good digital photograph.

7. Elementary **self-defense** techniques.

8. How to use your new laptop.

9. Lifesaving techniques of disaster **first aid**.

10. How to read **tarot** cards.

11. The basics of cross-country skiing, kayaking, or tennis.

15

ONE-SENTENCE **GUIDES TO**

GREAT BOOKS

THE ILIAD/Homer During siege of Troy, the arrogant yet powerful Achilles refuses to fight over a stolen woman, changes his mind after friend is killed.

HAMLET/Shakespeare Angsty Danish prince broods, seemingly goes crazy, and kills many, including his uncle, who had killed his father and married his mother.

KING LEAR/Shakespeare King Lear tries to retire by giving land away to his three daughters, who then cast him out, homeless and penniless, into a heath; chaos and much death ensue.

PRIDE & PREJUDICE/Jane Austen Elizabeth is prejudiced against snobby high society; wealthy Mr. Darcy is too proud to think Elizabeth is his equal; eventually, they get over themselves, romance, and marry.

FRANKENSTEIN/Mary Shelley Ambitious, yet misled, science student creates a human from cadavers, then abandons creation, who summarily kills everyone in creator's life.

JANE EYRE/Charlotte Brontë Orphan Jane falls in love with employer Mr. Rochester while working as governess to his ward, but it turns out he's got a crazy wife locked in the attic.

WUTHERING HEIGHTS/Emily Brontë Catherine and her wild adopted brother Heathcliff locked in passionate but doomed love on the moors.

GREAT EXPECTATIONS/Charles Dickens Spunky young orphan is saved from poverty through the generosity of a mysterious benefactor, seeks the love of a cold, yet striking, girl he had played with as a boy.

ANNA KARENINA/Leo Tolstoy Beautiful woman cheats on husband with dashing young military type, then after he moves on, throws self in front of train.

CRIME AND PUNISHMENT/Fyodor Dostoevsky Unstable and self-important young man murders old woman for kicks, feels guilty, turns self in.

PORTRAIT OF THE ARTIST AS A YOUNG MAN/James Joyce
Pensive boy grows up in Ireland, considers becoming priest, reconsiders after enjoying sex, becomes writer.

THE SUN ALSO RISES/Ernest Hemingway Group of listless lost-generationers mill around Europe, drink, fight bulls.

THE GREAT GATSBY/F. Scott Fitzgerald Charming yet mysterious Gatsby tries to win the love of patrician woman, who spurns Gatsby for her old-money husband, leading to Gatsby's death.

THE MAGIC MOUNTAIN/Thomas Mann Chummy young man visits cousin at Swiss tuberculosis sanatorium, is dubiously diagnosed with disease, stays seven years and listens to long-winded political arguments on eve of World War I.

TO THE LIGHTHOUSE/Virginia Woolf Selfless housewife deals with domestic duties, juggles social obligations, puts off taking son to lighthouse because of weather, dies.

10

NEUROBIC

NEUROBIC

EXERCISES

How to pump up your brain via novelty and sensory stimulation.

1. Trace a new route and try to drive it without consulting your map.

2. Trade houses or offices with a friend for an afternoon.

3. Rearrange a room where you spend a lot of time.

4. Hike a new route with a new friend.

5. Take a shower with your eyes closed.

6. Play a new game or work a new kind of puzzle.

7. Take your child or spouse somewhere you usually go alone.

8. Challenge yourself to read a new kind of book: history if you usually read contemporary romances, a classic or a book by a foreign author if you tend to self-help.

9. Prepare a meal with foods and recipes you've never used before.

10. Try a new creative activity: paint a watercolor, write the lyrics to a song, play the drums.

7

UNFATHOMABLE

CONCEPTS,

SIMPLIFIED

Conceptual Art Art in which the idea is more important than the aesthetics, as in Andy Warhol's soup cans.

Postmodernism A sweeping term applied to art, philosophy, and social movements that implies a rejection of modernism, or "a theory of rejecting theories."

Heisenberg's Uncertainty Principle The assertion that the act of observation changes the outcome, so that you can never be certain how a thing would behave if you weren't looking at it.

Reductionism A theory that says that the nature of a complex thing can be reduced to the nature of its simpler components basically, that everything is a sum of its parts.

Slow Food A movement in reaction to fast food that seeks to pre-serve regional cuisine and encourage locally produced food.

Bipolar A psychiatric disorder characterized by extreme mood swings. The definition has been expanded to encompass everything from manic-depression to feeling cranky in the morning, euphoric by lunch.

Ecosexual When being green is essential to being hot.

4

UNPROUNCEABLE

NAMES,

CLARIFIED

J.M. Coetzee/Nobel Prize–winning author There are nearly as many pronunciations for this South African writer's last name as there are citations of him on the web, but the general agreement is for cut-SEE-uh.

Brett Favre/legendary quarterback Pronounced fahrv, as if the r and the v were transposed. Don't ask us why: We're still trying to understand first and ten.

Ben Bernanke/chairman of the Federal Reserve Bank
The last name has three syllables: Bur-NAYNK-ee.

Wislawa Szymborska/poet You don't have to have an unpronounceable name to win the Nobel, but it seems to help. This Polish female poet's name is pronounced vees-WA-va shim-BOR-ska.

5

EASY WAYS **TO KEEP UP WITH**

WORLD

EVENTS

1. Put a **news source** like Reuters.com or Yahoo News on your computer desktop so you keep abreast of the headlines.

2. Instead of spending a whole half hour watching the news, go to the home page of a network or news channel like CNN.

3. Set **Google Alerts** for issues of more obscure interest—Darfur, say, or the Pennsylvania state legislature—and get targeted stories sent to you.

4. Ask coworkers, lunch dates, or people you meet at parties to fill you in on news stories they've been following—it's a conversation starter, and you'll learn a lot in the process.

5. Subscribe to a weekly news magazine. It's an old-fashioned but efficient way to **glean the highlights**.

6

BIG WORDS

YOU CAN **TOSS AROUND**

Recherché (re-share-SHAY) So excessively refined it can be appreciated only by true connoisseurs. "That Stella McCartney blouse with the weird buttons is so recherché."

Unprepossessing (un-pree-po-SESS-ing) Not impressive in any obvious way. "He looks totally unprepossessing, but he's actually a billionaire."

Laconic (lah-KAH-nik) Using few words. "I asked him what he was thinking, but I still don't know since his answer was laconic."

Anthropomorphize (an-thro-po-MOR-fize) Attributing human characteristics to animals or objects. "She anthropomorphizes everything to the extent that she thinks her apartment feels lonely when she goes away for too long!"

Vernacular (ver-NAK-yoo-ler) The everyday language of a particular place. "When I went to Brooklyn, they said dees, dem, and dose – guess they were talking to me in the vernacular."

Idiosyncratic (i-dee-oh-sink-KRA-tik) Peculiar to an individual. "Don't order what I order; my taste in food is very idiosyncratic."

76 WAYS

TO BE A LITTLE MORE Successful at Work

5 Interview Musts

16 Smart Methods for Managing Your Boss

9 Ways to Create a More Effective To-Do List

8 Ways to Look Like You're Working Hard

7 Ways to Calm Your Nerves When Giving a Speech

11 Things to Negotiate If They Won't Give You a Raise

8 Times to Trust Your Gut

12 Good Reasons to Look for a New Job

INTERVIEW
MUSTS

1. **DRESS ONE NOTCH UP.** The old rule of wearing a suit to every interview may be passé, but find out what you can about the company's or business's culture and then dress one step up from how the person who's interviewing you will be dressed. If you're interviewing for a job at a Web company, for instance, where the boss is likely to be in jeans and a tee shirt, you wouldn't want to show up in a dress but you might throw a blazer over your tee shirt and wear boots instead of sneakers, as evidence that you both understand the rules and want to show respect.

2. **RESEARCH THE COMPANY.** In the age of Google, there's no excuse for not doing basic homework on the company: its size, products, relative health.

3. **ASK QUESTIONS.** Asking thoughtful questions shows you've been paying attention during the interview and that you're interested in the company.

4. **BE ENTHUSIASTIC.** You owe it to the interviewer to at least feign enthusiasm about the job and/or company you're applying to work at.

5. **WRITE A PERSONAL THANK YOU NOTE.** According to a businesswoman friend, a thoughtful, insightful thank you note—on paper, please, not via email—that reinforces the positives about the inteview works "like magic."

16

SMART METHODS **FOR MANAGING**
YOUR BOSS

The key to working smarter, not harder, is to manage up rather than down.

1. **UNDERSTAND YOUR BOSS'S GOALS AND PRESSURES.** Your job is to help him reach the goals and lighten the pressures.

2. **BRING HER SOLUTIONS, NOT PROBLEMS.** Rather than just dropping a problem in her lap, offer a way to solve it.

3. **DEAL WITH WHO HE IS, NOT WHO YOU WANT HIM TO BE.** Know and accept your boss for who he is rather than trying to change him.

4. **MAKE YOUR BOSS SHINE, BUT NOT AT YOUR OWN EXPENSE.** There's enough glory to go around.

5. **BE DEPENDABLE.** By being reliable in small ways—being on time, meeting deadlines—you win yourself freedom from your boss's micromanagement.

6. **ASK FOR CRITIQUES AND FEEDBACK.** Being open to your boss's opinion of your work, rather than defensive, can give you valuable information and help defuse tensions that might otherwise build up.

7. **OFFER POSITIVE FEEDBACK OF YOUR OWN.** Don't just confront your boss when you've got a problem, but catch her being good.

8. **MANAGE YOUR EMOTIONS.** You can't make him not yell, but you can make yourself not yell back or break down in tears.

9. **MAKE IT EASY FOR YOUR BOSS TO SUPPORT YOUR VISION.** Lay out your plans, do a good job on your projects, make her want to get behind you.

10. **KEEP HIM IN THE LOOP ABOUT WHATEVER YOU'RE DOING.** No memos that don't include him.

11. **UNDERSTAND ALL THE WAYS YOUR BOSS IS MANAGING UP.** It's vital to see how and when her decisions may not really be about her, but about her boss.

12. **DON'T GO OVER HIS HEAD.** Unless he's committing a crime.

13. **DEVELOP ALLIES.** If you want to move ahead or effect change, you'll need a team rather than looking for your boss to give you permission.

14. **DON'T GANG UP AGAINST YOUR BOSS.** Even if your boss is difficult, indulging in endless complaining with coworkers is toxic to your relationship with your boss and to the entire workplace.

15. **KNOW WHEN TO MOVE ON.** If your boss is truly impossible, it may be more productive to find a new boss.

16. **BUT NEVER TRASH THE BOSS.** It will ultimately reflect badly on you.

9

WAYS TO CREATE **A MORE EFFECTIVE**
TO-DO LIST

1. Scribble down everything you can imagine, from Do Laundry to Get MBA, on a master to-do list. Then sort into short-range and long-range projects, things that need to be done today and those that can wait, higher and lower priority items.

2. For big or long-range projects with a deadline far in the future, work backward to break down smaller tasks and create shorter deadlines.

3. Give high priority to things you want to do—write a novel—so they don't get lost among all the dozens of things you *have* to do.

4. If you're simultaneously trying to make progress on two or three big projects—launch a business, reorganize your house, and shepherd a pet charity, for instance—devote finite chunks of time every day to each and don't let them intrude upon each other. Set an alarm clock if you must.

5. Corral everything—to-do lists, notes, dates—in **one place,** whether it's a datebook, calendar, or computer file.

6. Put only as much as you can realistically accomplish on each day's list, so you don't get overwhelmed or feel defeated. Bigger, longer-range projects belong on longer-range lists, not on the **daily list.**

7. If something's stuck on your to-do list, you may need to break it into smaller, more doable steps. Rather than "Call accountant about tax return," for instance, you may need to delineate the steps you need to accomplish before you place the call: Gather receipts, for instance, and Look up accountant's phone number.

8. If something's *still* stuck on your to-do list, you may need to look at deeper reasons why you never tackle it or find alternate solutions: hire someone, enlist the help or advice of a friend, or decide you simply don't want to do it!

9. **Investigate** the wide range of free online tools designed to get and keep you organized, from more complicated social networking and organization tools such as myquire.com to simple list-makers such as gonutshell.com.

8

WAYS TO LOOK LIKE **YOU'RE WORKING**

HARD

1. Set your schedule by your boss's, coming in five minutes earlier and leaving five minutes later than she does.

2. Take notes while you're talking on the phone, even if you're chatting to your best friend about her date last night.

3. Always write a business lunch in your calendar, even if you're spending the time at the gym.

4. Ask your boss if you can call him on his cell on the weekend if you have questions about your project. He'll probably say no (but be impressed). And even if he says yes, all you have to do is ask the question, not actually spend your Saturday doing the work.

5. If you have to get up from your desk to get something, always walk briskly and purposefully.

6. Learn some minor but useful technical skill no one else knows.

7. Focus on productivity, not the amount of time you devote to something.

8. Emphasize the Big Idea: Giving yourself the time and space to think up innovative solutions and big-picture strategies will impress your boss.

7

WAYS TO CALM YOUR **NERVES**
WHEN GIVING A
SPEECH

1. Practice your speech on someone who loves you.

2. Wear something that always makes you feel confident.

3. Take a brisk walk, even if it's just through the hotel corridors, before you begin.

4. Don't worry about memorizing the talk—no one knows what you plan to say so you don't have to follow any script. Instead, write key words and phrases on index cards.

5. Find a few sympathetic faces in the audience to focus on.

6. If faces make you nervous, look at the back of the room. Everyone will think you're making eye contact with someone else.

7. When in doubt, talk slower and say less.

11

THINGS TO **NEGOTIATE IF THEY WON'T GIVE YOU A**

RAISE

1. An extra week's vacation.

2. A better title.

3. A part-time assistant.

4. Flexible hours.

5. A bonus if you meet your goals.

6. A commitment for a raise in the future.

7. A green light for a pet project.

8. Money to take a class that will help you move ahead.

9. Better benefits: more generous medical or dental, a 401k, a bigger expense account.

10. Expenses to go to a conference.

11. A sabbatical.

8

TIMES TO **TRUST YOUR**
GUT

1. When they lob you an unpredictable question in the middle of the interview.

2. When you're delivering a speech in front of 100 people and you forget what you were going to say next.

3. When your colleague points out that your top three buttons have come undone.

4. When your colleague makes a pass at you.

5. When the other side in a negotiation makes an offer you didn't anticipate.

6. When you suspect your assistant is sabotaging you.

7. When you suspect the guy at the next desk is making more money than you.

8. When you can tell your boss expects great things from you.

12

GOOD REASONS **TO LOOK FOR A**

NEW JOB

1. Your old assistant is now running your department.

2. You've become a **one-woman** corporate archives.

3. You don't dress, act, or think like anyone else at
   your company.

4. The **solution** to everything else that's wrong with your
   life—your relationship, your mood, your weight—would
   be to change jobs.

5. The idea of ever becoming your boss makes you want to
   run screaming for the hills.

6. All your former colleagues who've changed jobs are so
   much happier.

7. Whenever you ask for a raise or a promotion, the answer is no.

8. You had a nightmare about strangling your boss – and it wasn't the first time.

9. There are rumors your company is being sold or shut down, and you're pretty sure they're true.

10. There's something you're itching to do that you can't do where you are.

11. You dread Mondays, mornings, the end of any vacation.

12. You want to look for a new job, but you're scared.

SECTION ELEVEN

75 WAYS

TO ADD DOLLARS TO Your Net Worth

17 (Nearly) Painless Ways to Save $1,000 a Year

10 Really Useful Things to Do with a Dollar

9 Ways to Feel Richer Than You Are

21 Terms to Help You Fake Financial Savvy

8 Things That Are Worth Spending More For

10 Lessons from Mom on How to Meet a Rich Guy

17

(NEARLY) **PAINLESS WAYS**
TO SAVE
$1,000 **A YEAR**

1. Have money taken directly out of your paycheck or your checking account and deposited in savings.

2. Buy a beautiful **piggy bank** and throw in all your singles and change until it's full.

3. If you're an impulse shopper, make yourself **wait** at least 24 hours before making any purchase.

4. Maximize whatever matching savings your company offers.

5. Get Rid of cable, TiVO, Netflix, or even TV.

6. Cancel the gym membership and buy yourself some hand weights and **running shoes**.

7. Use only the doctors, dentists, and therapists on your insurance plan.

8. If you're trying to save money AND lose weight, you may find both answers in a single solution: Stop eating at restaurants!

9. Become a kamikaze grocery shopper, clipping coupons, stocking up on specials, buying in bulk, trolling the discounters.

10. Pay off all your credit cards—and then cut them up.

11. Weatherproof your house and turn down your thermostat.

12. Fire the cleaning lady, the lawn guy, and the Saturday night babysitter, and start swapping services with savings-minded friends.

13. Forget the expensive vacation house and take up camping.

14. Scour your insurance policies for savings you've overlooked: bigger deductibles, less coverage, discounts for good behavior.

15. Find and take all the tax deductions you're entitled to.

16. Declare one or two days per week spending-free, and then tuck the money you might have laid out on lattes and lunches into your savings account.

17. Put as much as possible into your retirement account, and save money in taxes now.

10

REALLY USEFUL **THINGS TO DO WITH**

A DOLLAR

1. Put one in a jar every day and at the end of the month pledge it to your favorite PBS station or food pantry.

2. Turn it in for 100 shiny pennies or 10 shiny dimes you scatter on the sidewalk for a lucky kid to find.

3. Buy a homeless person a cup of coffee.

4. Buy a more serious newspaper than you normally read and give yourself a crash course on current events.

5. Buy a postcard and stamp to get back in touch with an old friend.

6. Or call that old friend and talk on the phone for 20 minutes.

7. Leave a bigger-than-average tip and make a waitress's day.

8. Go to the 99-cent store and treat yourself to a CD of Celtic harp music or an iridescent martini glass.

9. Download the perfect song to rev up your workout, day after day.

10. Jumpstart your diet with an irresistible piece of exotic fruit.

9

WAYS TO **FEEL**

RICHER

THAN **YOU ARE**

1. Drink your water out of a crystal goblet and use the real silver at every meal.

2. **Double** whatever you were going to tip.

3. Buy the top-of-the-line version of something small: the pint of ice cream, the basic white panty.

4. Spring for the valet parking.

5. Get the kind of bank account that gives you a free safe deposit box. No one has to know you only keep your baby pictures there.

6. **Buy bonds** for your IRA.

7. Read a secrets-of-the-rich-and-famous book, anything from *The Great Gatsby* to *Bergdorf Blondes*.

8. Spend the day at a **spa.**

9. Lounge in the lobby of the fanciest hotel in town.

21

TERMS TO **HELP YOU FAKE**

FINANCIAL

SAAVY

AMORTIZATION The repayment of a loan via pre-calculated payments that include both principal and interest.

ARM That's right, it's pronounced just like the one attached to your shoulder. But it stands for Adjustable Rate Mortgage, one that has an interest rate that changes at specified intervals over the life of the loan, up to a predetermined cap.

COMPOUNDING One reason the rich get richer: their money earns interest, and then their interest earns more interest.

529 PLAN A savings plan whose earnings are tax-free if used for education.

FRONT-END LOAD A sales charge that's paid when you buy an investment (as opposed to when you sell it).

GROWTH FUND A mutual fund that specializes in stocks with growth potential.

JUNK BOND A bond that pays a high interest rate but also has a high potential to crash.

KEOGH ACCOUNT Retirement plan for self-employed people or unincorporated businesses.

LONG-TERM CAPITAL GAINS TAX If you hold an investment longer than a year, you pay this lower tax rate—generally 15 percent—on any money it earns.

MARGIN ACCOUNT A brokerage account you can borrow from to buy securities, using securities you already own as collateral.

MUNI Nickname for a municipal bond issued by a city or state that pays interest but is usually exempt from some or all taxes.

NASDAQ Acronym for the National Association of Securities Dealers Automated Quotation System, which trades stocks—many of them from the high-tech world—electronically rather than on an actual trading floor.

OPTION A contract that lets you buy or sell a stock at a certain price by a specific date. A buy option is a "call" and a sell option is a "put."

PITI Acronym for Principle, Interest, Taxes, and Insurance— which add up to the elements of a mortgage payment.

POINTS Upfront fees that reduce the interest rate of a loan. One point equals one percent of the total amount of a loan—in other words, $1000 on a $100,000 mortgage.

P/E Short for price/earnings ratio, the price of a stock compared with its per-share earnings, usually used to determine whether it's a sound investment. A stock selling for $10 a share with earnings of $1 a share, for example, would have a p/e ratio of 10. In general, the lower the p/e ratio, the more desirable.

ROTH IRA A special retirement account available only to those with incomes under a certain amount that allows tax-free withdrawals before retirement age for certain purposes, such as education.

SELLING SHORT Betting on a stock to go down rather than up.

S & P 500 Short for Standard & Poor's 500 Stock Index, a common index of 500 stocks used to measure performance.

TERM INSURANCE Life insurance that stays in effect only for a specified period of time—10 or 20 years, for instance—or until you reach a certain age.

ZERO COUPON BOND A bond that pays no interest but that you buy at a deep discount, collecting the face value only when it matures.

8

THINGS THAT ARE **WORTH**

SPENDING

MORE FOR

1. A designer suit if you're going after a big job.

2. Blue chip stocks.

3. A car that's comfortable, safe, and problem-free for 100,000 miles.

4. Orchestra seats.

5. A bra.

6. Champagne.

7. Pillows.

8. A dentist.

10

LESSONS **FROM**

MOM

ON HOW TO MEET A **RICH GUY**

1. Eat, drink, and be merry in the financial district.

2. Forget bowling: Take up golf, polo, fox-hunting.

3. Volunteer to run a charity ball.

4. Switch careers and become a fund-raiser or a high-level money manager.

5. Go for your MBA or law degree.

6. Join the Republican Party.

7. Cultivate a male-oriented high-priced hobby: flying, wine collecting.

8. Wear expensive clothes and shoes.

9. Refine your etiquette and your elocution.

10. Don't talk about money.

79 WAYS

TO MAKE THE WORLD a Slightly Better Place

9

TECHNIQUES FOR
RAISING

MONEY

**THAT DON'T
INVOLVE A
BAKE SALE**

1. Auction or raffle high-ticket services that the members of your organization might provide: catering a party, critiquing a manuscript.

2. Ask a local store to donate a percentage of a designated item to your cause.

3. Ask a local store to loan clothes for a benefit fashion show.

4. Host a talent show: the more outrageous the talent, the more profitable the evening.

5. Organize a tour of the best kitchens or gardens in your town.

6. Hold a spelling bee, asking teams to find sponsors to donate money for each word they spell correctly.

7. Throw a kids-against-the-grownups or men-against-the-women contest—basketball game, battle of the bands—and sell tickets.

8. Sell seasonal items at a steep markup: mums in the fall, herbs in the spring.

9. Host individual parties with appealing themes—a father-daughter brunch, say, or a makeover evening—that combine fundraising with pleasure.

THINGS

YOU

CAN DO
FOR YOUR
COMMUNITY
IN UNDER
AN HOUR

1. **Read** a book at a Head Start center or a kindergarten class.

2. Show off a talent at a nursing home.

3. Show up at a town meeting and **contribute** your opinion.

4. Plant flowers in a public place.

5. Make phone calls in support of a candidate or cause you believe in.

6. Organize a block party or progressive dinner to bring your neighbors together.

7. Organize dinner **contributions** for a friend who's sick or who's just had a baby.

8. Email colleagues about forming a professional or civic organization.

9. **Mentor** a high school kid who wants to go into your field.

10. Tutor a new immigrant in English or a third-grader in math.

11. Treat an elderly neighbor who may be lonely to lunch.

18

DOWN-TO-EARTH **WAYS TO HELP THE**

ENVIRONMENT

1. Buy **energy-efficient** appliances.

2. Use compact fluorescent bulbs, especially in places where you leave lights burning: the front porch, for instance, or the laundry room.

3. Buy bulk-size products to **save** packaging.

4. Use electric razors over disposables.

5. Clean with nontoxic products.

6. When possible, use paper instead of plastic, cloth instead of paper.

7. Inflate your tires and change your air filter to maximize auto fuel performance.

8. Lower your **thermostat**—and don't forget to do the same on your water heater.

9. Unplug appliances when not in use.

10. Recycle.

11. Buy recycled products.

12. Bring your own bags – fabric, string, or reused plastic – to the supermarket.

13. Tell companies to stop sending catalogs and instead order online.

14. Rather than throwing out clothes, books, household goods, or unwanted gifts, hold a swap party.

15. Opt out of junk mail by filling out the form at directmail.com or dmaconsumers.org.

16. Switch to low-flow showerheads and toilets.

17. Drive fuel-efficient vehicles.

18. When possible, take public transportation or better yet, bike or walk.

8

THINGS YOU NEVER **KNEW YOU COULD** DONATE

1. YOUR OLD PROM GEAR New and almost new formal wear for girls heading to proms in Chicago can be donated to the Glass Slipper Project at glassslipperproject.org, along with your services as a personal fashion advisor to girls shopping the charity's boutiques.

2. A CUT OF YOUR EBAY PROCEEDS Donate a portion of the proceeds of everything you sell on eBay to the nonprofit of your choice via Mission Fish at missionfish.org.

3. YOUR WEDDING GIFTS Already have two toasters? Instead of standard gifts, register to receive donations in your name at justgive.org.

4. THE OFFICE FAX Donate computers and office electronics via recycles.org.

5. YOUR HAIR Give your hair to make a wig for a child who's lost hers through locksoflove.org.

6. YOUR OLD CELL PHONE Cell phones are recycled for women's shelters via shelteralliance.net.

7. YOUR TIME SHARE Many charities accept time shares as contributions. One such organization: nfcr.org.

8. YOUR BONE MARROW To donate your bone marrow or register to be matched, see marrow.org or abmdr.org.

10

CHARITIES **WORTH GIVING**

$100

(OR MORE) **TO**

There are hundreds of worthy charities in the U.S. – and hundreds of unworthy ones, too. To tell which are worth your donation, go to charitynavigator.org or give.org, for ratings and a complete rundown of how they spend their money. Some better-known charities that meet the criteria and may appeal to your values include:

AMERICAN CIVIL LIBERTIES UNION FOUNDATION Protects civil rights. 125 Broad Street, 18th floor, NY, NY 10004 212-549-2500 aclu.org

AMERICAN LUNG ASSOCIATION Lung health and antismoking programs. 61 Broadway, NY, NY 10006 800-586-4872 lungusa.org

HEIFER PROJECT INTERNATIONAL Sends livestock to poor people worldwide. One World Avenue, Little Rock, AR 72202 800-422-0474 heifer.org

NATURAL RESOURCES DEFENSE COUNCIL Environmental protection group. 40 West 20th Street, NY, NY 10011 212-727-2700 nrdc.org

THE NEW-YORK HISTORICAL SOCIETY Preserves New York history. 170 Central Park West, NY, NY 10024 212-873-3400 nyhistory.org

THE OVARIAN CANCER RESEARCH FUND Funding research for a cure. 14 Pennsylvania Plaza, Suite 1400, NY, NY 10122 800-873-9569 ocrf.org

PLANNED PARENTHOOD Offers free and low-cost family planning services. 434 West 33rd Street, NY, NY 10001 800-798-7092 plannedparenthood.org

SAVE THE CHILDREN International children's relief fund. 54 Wilton Road, Westport, CT 06880 800-728-3843 savethechildren.org

THE SPHINX ORGANIZATION Builds diversity in classical music. 400 Renaissance Center, Suite 2550, Detroit, MI 48243 313-877-9100 sphinxmusic.org

WOMEN'S SPORTS FOUNDATION Supports women in sports. Eisenhower Park, East Meadow, NY 11554 800-227-3988 womenssportsfoundation.org

1

BEST CAUSE **FOR YOUR TIME AND**
MONEY

The best charity for you will usually be a local one whose impact you can see in your community: the soup kitchen that has a tireless director and a long line at its door every week, the school library that works double-time to get kids reading, the church that supports a wide range of causes. If your town offers no such organization, you might find the most satisfaction in donating to a cause to which you have a personal relationship: the alma mater you loved, the foundation that researches a disease that afflicts someone dear to you.

10

IDEAS FOR A **GREENER HOLIDAY**

SEASON

1. Buy recycled wrapping papers and reusable gift bags.

2. Recycle packing peanuts.

3. Give nonmaterial gifts: tickets, food, cash.

4. For dress-up gear and holiday decorations, buy vintage.

5. If you're throwing a party, rent or buy real tableware and linens rather than using disposable goods.

6. Minimize holiday lights to conserve energy.

7. Use rechargeable batteries in kids' gifts.

8. Send ecards and invitations rather than paper.

9. Buy a live tree that can be planted after the holiday.

10. Spend the holidays in your own neighborhood; not driving after holiday parties is safer and better for the environment.

4

ANONYMOUS
WAYS TO DO
GOOD

1. Send a hundred-dollar bill to a worthy person you read about in the newspaper.

2. Adopt a family to buy Christmas presents for.

3. Drop extra bills in the collection plate at church.

4. Send money to a charity in someone else's name.

8

WAYS TO MAKE THE
WORLD A TINY BIT MORE
BEAUTIFUL

1. Plant flowers in a window box: long-blooming impatiens grow in even the shadiest spot.

2. Sow wildflower seeds by the side of the road.

3. Pick up litter in a park or by the side of the road.

4. Paint a little girl's toenails.

5. Plant a butterfly bush to attract a yardful of beautiful creatures.

6. Organize a community garden.

7. Give to a tree-planting organization: a highly rated one is the World Forestry Center at worldforestry.org.

8. Laugh!